THIS CANDLEWICK BOOK BELONGS TO:

_____

_____

_____

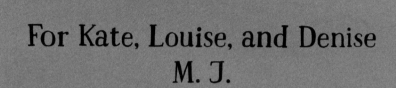

For Kate, Louise, and Denise
M. J.

For Mum and Dad
R. J.

This is a book about a bird, and it is also a book
about forces. As you read this book with a child,
you may want to discuss the following concepts:

A force is something that changes an object's motion;
it can make an object stop or start moving,
move faster or slower, or change direction.

More force is needed to change the motion of heavier objects
than to change the motion of lighter objects.

Gravity is a force that pulls objects toward one another.
Earth's gravity pulls objects toward the Earth, which
makes things fall down when they are dropped.

Bird
Builds
a Nest

Martin Jenkins

illustrated by
Richard Jones

It's a beautiful day!
Bird is up early—
she's got a lot to do.

First she needs some breakfast.

What she wants is a nice, juicy . . .

worm.

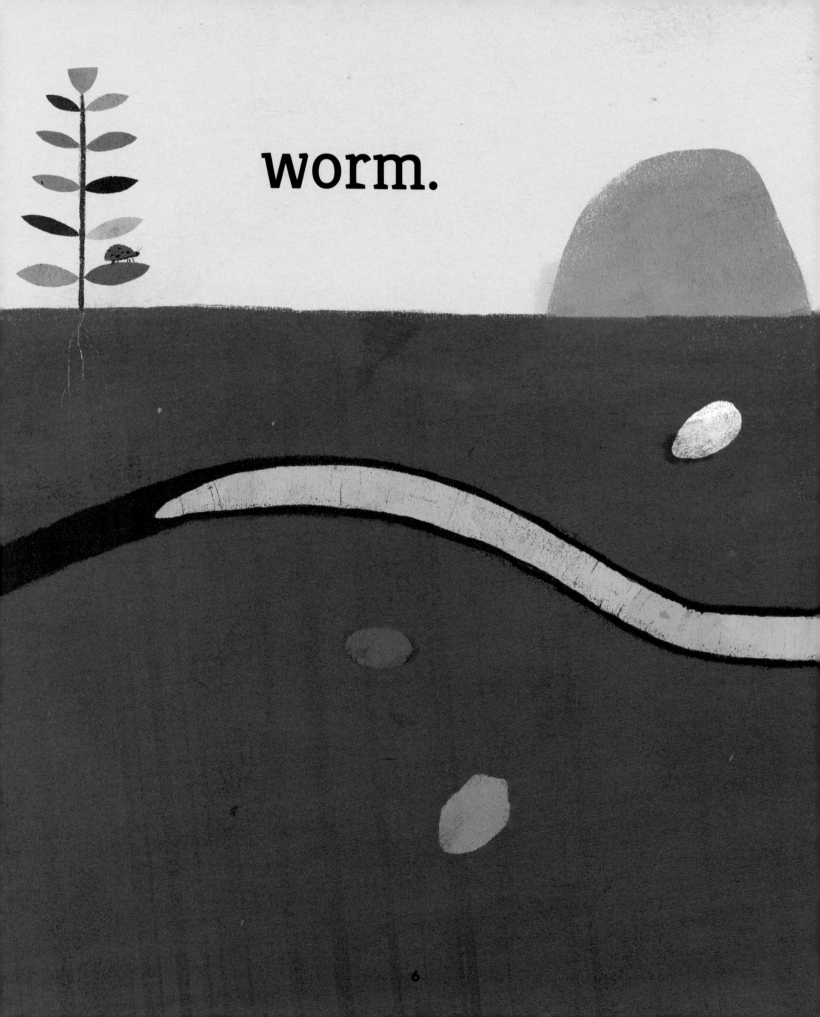

Bird pulls hard, but
the worm pulls back.

It's a big worm,
and it's strong.

Too strong for Bird.

Ah. This one's better.

It's smaller and not as strong. Delicious!

Now Bird can get on with her work.

She's not looking for worms now.

She needs twigs. Lots of twigs.

This one's too
heavy.

And so is this one.

All of these will do fine.

Bird can carry
one large twig

or two medium-size twigs

or three or four small twigs
(although it's hard to fit
that many in her beak at once).

She's building her nest.
It's not quite finished, though.
Carefully, she pushes a twig into the side of
the nest and pulls its end back out.

Pushing and pulling, she gets all
the twigs in place.

She works for hours,

fetching and carrying,

flying back and forth,

pushing and pulling.

Sometimes she drops a twig, but it doesn't matter.

She's looking for softer
things now: dried grass and feathers.
They're very light. She can carry
lots of these at once.

She tucks them into place.

Turning around and around,
pushing with her whole body,

she makes a snug little cup,
smooth and soft on the inside.

The nest is ready and waiting.

Can you guess what it's waiting for?

Eggs!
Five of them, speckled and beautiful
and getting ready to hatch.

THINKING ABOUT
PUSHING AND PULLING

When you try to move something away from you, it's called pushing.
Can you find some places in the book where Bird pushes something?

When you try to move something toward you, it's called pulling.
Can you find some places in the book where Bird pulls something?

Heavy things are hard for Bird to move. Can you name
three things that are too heavy for you to move?

Light things are easy for Bird to move. Can you name
three things that are light enough for you to move?

What happens when Bird drops a twig?
Try dropping a small object, like a pencil.
A force called gravity pulls it toward the ground!

INDEX

Look up the pages to find out about forces.

First U.S. paperback edition 2020

Library of Congress Catalog Card Number 2018933643
ISBN 978-0-7636-9346-6 (hardcover)
ISBN 978-1-5362-1056-9 (paperback)

22 23 24 CCP 10 9 8 7 6 5 4

Printed in Shenzhen, Guangdong, China

This book was typeset in Kreon.
The illustrations were done in mixed media.

Candlewick Press
99 Dover Street
Somerville, Massachusetts 02144

visit us at www.candlewick.com

CANDLEWICK PRESS

Martin Jenkins has written many celebrated books for children, including *Fox Explores the Night: A First Science Storybook*, illustrated by Richard Smythe; *The Squirrels' Busy Year: A First Science Storybook*, illustrated by Richard Jones; *The Emperor's Egg*, illustrated by Jane Chapman; and *Can We Save the Tiger?*, illustrated by Vicky White. Martin Jenkins lives in England, where he also works as a conservation biologist.

Richard Jones is an illustrator with more than fifteen years' experience in the creative arts. He lives in England.